KIDS!
PARTY FOOD

KÖNEMANN

Planning a party

When it's time for your child's birthday party, a little forward planning will help to make the very special day a great success. Whether the party is to be a simple morning tea for toddlers, a full scale, dress-up extravaganza for sixteen six-year-olds or a sleep-over for pre-teens, work out the relevant details beforehand with the guest-of-honour.

A few weeks before the date, decide where your party will be held, what kind of party, how long it will last and how many guests to invite. Your child should draw up the guest list; even young children have definite ideas on who they want to ask, and what type of party they would like to have. If you can't cope with a large number, say so at the beginning and give your child a number to work with, for example six or 10 guests. A small group of happy children can form the basis of a terrific party.

Food

Supply plenty of food and drink – children find parties hungry and thirsty work – and a variety of savoury and sweet foods, both warm and cold, so that fussy guests can have a choice. Keep the food interesting with a blend of crunchy, soft and hard textures, and a good mix of flavours.

When making up the menu, plan on serving four to six different savoury dishes (hot and cold) plus two to three sweet dishes, including one chilled or frozen dish, plus the birthday cake. Offer two different cool drinks.

When you have chosen the menu, make a shopping list and decide which tasks can be done beforehand and what to do on the day.

Special Note

When planning party food for young children, avoid nuts and hard sweets, toothpicks and other sharp objects.

Very small children appreciate party food that is easy to hold and won't crumble or collapse. Use sturdy, plastic cups and plates as they are easier for little hands to grip; half-fill to avoid spills.

At parties, toddlers will tend to "graze", snatching a bite or two of food between play, while older kids will sit down, load their plate and speedily consume a surprising amount of food! All kids love colourful and imaginative food – especially familiar food dressed up, while cheerful napkins and tablecloth add to the party atmosphere.

Venue

Parties don't have to be at home. Depending on the time of year, parks, zoos, amusement parks, water works, beach or bush all offer alternative spaces for a party. A child's hobby could suggest a venue, such as a picnic and riding at a horse-riding school, or kite flying at the breeziest park around.

Balloons can help to

make your party easy to find. For parties at home, tie a bunch of balloons and streamers to the front gate; outdoors, tie a big, bright bunch to the nearest tree.

Invitations

Party invitations can be bought or you can make your own. Write them out (or better still, let the birthday boy or girl) in coloured pens on stiff paper, giving all the essential information – name, address, arrival and departure times, and theme. Give directions or a simple map for any hard-to-find places and a phone number to RSVP.

Personalised montage invitations are easy and fun to make. Cut out pictures or photographs from magazines, such as famous people, pop stars or animals, arrange them with a photograph of the birthday boy or girl and photocopy them onto, or glue them to coloured paper. Colour or brush with glue and sprinkle with glitter.

Parties for kids aged 1 to 6

For very little ones, invite parents along as well – toddlers need help and more attention than one or two adults can give. The simplest party is a morning or afternoon tea for parents and children with phone invitations.

Kids love imaginatively presented food. (See p. 44.)

Hold the party in the garden so there is no worry about spills. Pick a shady spot and spread out a blanket for the babies. Clean up the garden, making sure it's quite safe for inquisitive little people and for your peace of mind put anything precious out of sight and reach.

For energetic toddlers, a party lasting about two hours with five or six guests is suitable.

Two-year-olds and under won't need organised games, but will like to play in the sandpit or with toys (make sure there are plenty to go around).

For kids from four to six years, simple, fun games can be arranged, and older children may like to help littler ones.

Parties for kids aged 7 to 12

This is the peak age for birthday parties. Older children will enjoy helping with planning and ideas, and may lend a hand with food and making decorations.

A garden party with around 10 guests and lasting three hours will provide plenty of fun but parties away from home save on mess, and ensure plenty of space for energetic playing. Remember, girls and boys around this age often have very different ideas about what makes a party fun.

Traditional tried-and-true party games with balloons, balls, treasure-hunts, pass-the-parcel, musical cushions, etc, remain strong favourites. If the party has a theme, adapt the food, games and prizes to suit.

Keep the party moving. Make a timetable for activities and games and set aside a time for eating and for the cake cutting – but don't worry if things don't go entirely to plan.

Even big kids like to take home a "goody bag" packed with sweets and novelties and perhaps a piece of the birthday cake. Keep them hidden until it's time for guests to leave.

Easy to eat and delicious savoury food. (See p. 12.)

Themes
Simple ideas, such as a silly hat party or a mask party, can be quite as successful as full-blown themes.

Decide how much time and effort you can spare – you may like to invite all the guests to dress up and decorate a room or two, or confine your theme to the tea table and birthday cake.

Fancy-dress parties are a great idea, but check with the children before you become too enthused – some kids grow out of dressing up or may feel shy. Also, making decorations or costumes can be great fun, but takes time, energy and money and

may be out of the question for some busy working parents.

Many old favourites, such as pirate or cowboy parties, are still popular, yet party themes are really only limited by your imagination.

Take the children to space with an Outer Limits party, featuring dressed-up aliens and astronauts and lots of "space food". Hold a Witch, Wizard & Warlock Convention, or host a Teddy Bears' Picnic in the backyard or park, where every child brings a bear and goes on a treasure hunt for the "honeypot" filled with goodies. "Bug" parties, where spiders and worms turn up in the non-scary form of drinks, cakes and meringues, are fun for younger children.

A party can be based around a movie, book or comic book, with guests dressing as their favourite characters. Little ones love to transform themselves into animals, clowns, fairies, cowboys/girls, superheroes, flowers, aliens and characters from fairy tales.

For pre-teens, set up their own disco party, featuring the music of the current favourite pop and rock groups. Serve mini-burgers, hot dogs and shakes in your own "Rock Cafe".

If the weather is unsuitable for outdoor

entertaining, base the party around a favourite movie. Show it on the video, with old and new cartoons – most video stores have a good variety. Serve popcorn and finger food.

Pyjama parties are fun – sleeping over is

very popular; all boys or all girls being the usual rule. Set aside a large room or a tent or tents in the garden. Make a time for lights out. Guests can bring torches, toothbrushes, sleeping bags and nightwear. Serve a special late-night supper of pikelets and hot chocolate.

In summer, backyard pool parties are good for older children, but all ages love to splash about in water. Under the watchful eye of parents, a shallow wading pool with a little water and floating toys will be a hit with the toddlers.

Decorations
Adapt ideas to suit your circumstances. Party supply shops have a large range of ready-made decorations, noisemakers, helium balloons and costumes for all kinds of parties. For do-it-yourself party givers, raid the local discount fabric shop and big chain stores for lengths of inexpensive materials such as calico, 150 cm-wide sheeting, bright cheap cottons or remants and samples to create your decorations. Lengths of black plastic can drape a room for a spooky effect and netting comes in many colours and can be used

for everything from costumes to imitation spider webs. Crêpe paper and felt are inexpensive and very adaptable for costumes and decorations.

Whatever you decide to do for your party, organise ahead and you'll be able to relax and have fun on the day.

Party Preparation

Two weeks before:

☆ Make guest list.

☆ Send out the invitations.

☆ Plan the menu. Make a list of everything you need to buy.

☆ Plan the decorations. Make a list of everything you need to buy or make.

☆ Mark in your diary or make a timetable for preparatory tasks and do-ahead cooking.

☆ Make a timetable for the party.

☆ Recruit help.

Savoury Surprises

The children's party table becomes an exciting adventure with these simply prepared and fabulous-to-eat dishes. Combine old favourites with bright new ideas, such as mini-size burgers, pizzas, spring rolls and meatballs. Tie cheese sticks up in knots, go Asian with spring rolls and satay or give guests a happy surprise with food disguised as boats or bon-bons. Protect the table with a bright cloth and supply plenty of napkins and good-sized, sturdy plates.

Frankfurt Bon-Bons

Preparation Time:
  20 minutes
Cooking Time:
  15 minutes
Makes 12

12 *small cocktail frankfurts*
3 *sheets ready-rolled puff pastry*
1 *egg, lightly beaten*
cotton or jute string

1 Preheat oven to moderate 180°C. Line two 32 x 28 cm oven trays with aluminium foil. Brush with melted butter or oil.
2 Prick frankfurts with a fork. Cut each pastry sheet into 4 squares. Brush each square with beaten egg. Place a frankfurt on each pastry sheet at the edge, roll up. Press edge lightly to seal.
3 Carefully pinch the pastry together, about 1.5 cm in from edge. Tie loosely with pieces of string. Using scissors, cut a fringe from the edge almost to the string.
4 Place bon-bons onto the prepared trays; brush lightly with the beaten egg. Bake 15 minutes or until golden.

HINT
For a strong display, present party food on large platters or trays. Bowls of dipping sauce can be placed directly on the platter.

Baby Burgers (top), Frankfurt Bon-Bons (bottom).

Baby Burgers

Preparation Time:
  30 minutes
Cooking Time:
  10 minutes
Makes 10

500 g beef mince
1 small onion, finely
  chopped
1 tablespoon finely
  chopped parsley
1 egg, lightly beaten
1 tablespoon tomato
  sauce
1/2 teaspoon herb
  pepper seasoning
2 tablespoons oil
10 small bread rolls,
  halved

Topping
2 cups finely shredded
  lettuce
2 small tomatoes, thinly
  sliced
1 Lebanese cucumber,
  thinly sliced
  lengthways
5 rings canned
  pineapple, drained
  and halved
5 cheese slices, halved
tomato or barbecue
  sauce

1 Combine the mince,
onion, parsley, beaten
egg, tomato sauce and
herb pepper seasoning
in a large bowl. Using
hands, mix until well
combined. Divide the
mixture into 10 portions.
Shape into round patties.

2 Heat oil in a large
heavy-based pan over
medium heat. Cook the
patties 5 minutes each
side, or until they are well
browned. Remove and
drain on absorbent paper.
3 To assemble burgers,
place a patty onto each
roll. Top with lettuce,
tomato, cucumber and
a pineapple and cheese
slice. Finish with sauce
and top with remaining
rolls. Serve immediately.

Kid-Style Nachos

Preparation Time:
  15 minutes
Cooking Time:
  10 minutes
Serves 6-8

150 g packet corn chips
1 cup grated tasty
  Cheddar cheese
2 medium tomatoes,
  finely chopped
2 tablespoons finely
  chopped spring onions

1 Preheat oven to
moderate 180°C. Line a
baking tray with foil.
2 Arrange corn chips in
a single layer over the
prepared tray. Sprinkle
with cheese, tomatoes
and spring onion. Bake
10 minutes or until the
cheese is melted and
golden. Let Nachos cool
slightly before serving.

Prawn Toasts

Preparation Time:
  15 minutes
Cooking Time:
  15 minutes
Makes 32

375 g medium green
  king prawns
1 egg
1/2 teaspoon lemon
  pepper seasoning
1 teaspoon onion flakes
1 spring onion, chopped
8 slices white bread

1 Preheat oven to
moderate 180°C. Line
two 32 x 28 cm oven
trays with foil.
2 Peel and devein the
prawns. Place prawns,
egg, seasoning, onion
flakes and spring onion
in food processor bowl.
Using the pulse action,
press button 30 seconds
or until the mixture is
smooth and lump-free.
3 Spread evenly over
bread. Cut crusts from
bread and cut each slice
into 4 triangles. Place
onto the prepared trays.
Bake 15 minutes or
until golden and slightly
puffed. Serve warm.

Note: Uncooked Prawn
Toasts can be frozen for
3-4 weeks. It is not
necessary to thaw them
before cooking.

Kid-Style Nachos (top), Prawn Toasts (bottom).

Pinwheel Kebabs

Preparation Time:
 20 minutes
Cooking Time:
 Nil
Makes 10

8 slices bread
100 g can red salmon,
 drained
2 teaspoons mayonnaise
2 teaspoons finely
 chopped fresh chives
yeast extract, optional
4 cheese slices
1/2 cup shredded lettuce

1 Remove crusts from
the bread. Combine the
salmon, mayonnaise and
chives in a small mixing
bowl. Stir until smooth.
Spread 4 slices of bread
with salmon mixture.
Roll up bread; cut into
1.5 cm slices.
2 Spread yeast extract,
if using, on remaining
bread. Top with cheese
slices and lettuce. Roll
up bread; slice as before.
3 To serve, alternately
thread the salmon and
the cheese and lettuce
wheels onto skewers.

Corny Cheese Row Boats

Preparation Time:
 25 minutes
Cooking Time:
 10 minutes
Makes 24

40 g butter
1 tablespoon plain flour
1/2 cup milk
1/4 cup grated Cheddar
 cheese
1/4 teaspoon chicken
 stock powder
130 g can corn kernels,
 drained
herb pepper
24 savoury boat shells
24 straight pretzels,
 halved

1 Heat butter in a
medium heavy-based
pan; add flour. Stir over
low heat for 1 minute or
until lightly golden.
2 Add milk gradually
to the pan, stirring until
smooth. Stir constantly
over medium heat for
5 minutes or until the
mixture boils and
thickens. Boil 1 minute
more; remove from
heat. Stir in the grated
cheese, stock powder,
corn and pepper to taste.
3 Spoon 3 teaspoons of
mixture into each pastry
boat. Arrange pretzels
as oars. Serve warm.

Corny Cheese Row Boats (top),
Pinwheel Kebabs (bottom).

1. *For Sausage Rolls: Combine mince, onion, egg, sauces and breadcrumbs.*

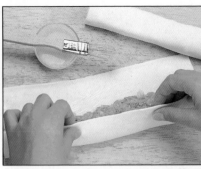

2. *Place mince mixture on pastry. Roll up and press edges to seal.*

Sausage Rolls

Preparation Time:
  40 minutes
Cooking Time:
  25 minutes
Makes 40

250 g sausage mince
1 small onion, finely
  chopped
1 egg, lightly beaten
1 tablespoon barbecue
  sauce
2 teaspoons
  Worcestershire sauce
1/3 cup breadcrumbs
2 sheets ready-rolled
  puff pastry
1 egg, lightly beaten,
  extra

1 Preheat oven to moderate 180°C. Line two 32 x 28 cm baking trays with aluminium foil. Brush trays with melted butter or oil.
2 Combine the mince, onion, egg, sauces and breadcrumbs in a large bowl. Using hands, mix until well combined.
3 Cut pastry sheets in half lengthways. Brush with extra beaten egg. Divide mince mixture into 4 portions. Place one portion lengthways down the centre of each pastry sheet. Roll up and press edges to seal.
4 With the seam-side down, make 9 slices in each roll, almost cutting through and leaving the base attached. Using a long knife, carefully lift the sausage rolls onto prepared trays. Brush with extra egg. Bake 25 minutes or until pastry is golden and crisp.
5 Cut into individual sausage rolls. Serve hot.

Note: Substitute beef or lamb mince for sausage mince, if preferred. Serve with tomato sauce.

Sausage Rolls.

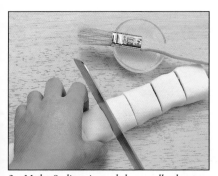

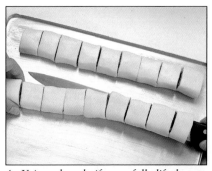

3. *Make 9 slices in each long roll, almost cutting through.*

4. *Using a long knife, carefully lift the sausage rolls onto prepared trays.*

Chicken Pocket Cones

Preparation Time:
  20 minutes
Cooking Time:
  Nil
Makes 8

2 small round pita
  breads
2 tablespoons cheese
  spread
2 tablespoons
  mayonnaise
4 slices chicken loaf,
  halved
chives, for tying cones
1 cup finely shredded
  lettuce
1 small tomato, finely
  chopped
1 small Lebanese
  cucumber,
  finely chopped

1 Cut each pita bread
in half. Split halves to
make 8 semi-circles.
Spread evenly with the
cheese spread and the
mayonnaise. Top with a
piece of the chicken loaf.
2 Roll each semi-circle
into a cone. Tie with a
chive to hold the shape.
3 Combine the lettuce,
tomato and cucumber
in a bowl. Fill the top
of each cone with salad.
Make Chicken Cones up
to 1 hour before serving.
Store in refrigerator.

Cowboy Dogs

Preparation Time:
  10 minutes
Cooking Time:
  5 minutes
Makes 16

4 frankfurts
8 hot dog buns
225 g can baked beans
100 g grated Cheddar
  cheese

1 Heat the frankfurts
by placing in simmering
water for 3 minutes.
Cut the hot dog buns in
half lengthways; hollow
out the centre, leaving
base and sides about
1.5 cm thick.
2 Cut the frankfurts
into 2 cm pieces; divide
equally between bread
shells. Cover with baked
beans and sprinkle
evenly with grated
cheese. Place under a hot
grill and cook until the
cheese has melted and is
golden brown. Leave to
cool for 2 minutes. Serve
with a large paper
napkin to catch drips.

Ham and Pineapple Pinwheels

Preparation Time:
  25 minutes
Cooking Time:
  15 minutes
Makes about 30

2 sheets ready-rolled
  puff pastry
1 egg, lightly beaten
100 g ham, thinly sliced
150 g tinned crushed
  pineapple, well drained
1/3 cup grated Cheddar
  cheese

1 Preheat oven to
moderate 180°C. Line
two 32 x 28 cm oven
trays with aluminium
foil. Brush trays with
melted butter or oil.
2 Lay out pastry sheets;
brush with beaten egg.
Sprinkle evenly with the
ham, pineapple and
cheese. Press gently.
3 Roll each sheet up
firmly and evenly. Using
a sharp serrated or
electric knife, cut each
roll into 10 rounds.
Place pinwheels on the
prepared trays allowing
room for spreading.
Bake for 15 minutes or
until golden and puffed.
Serve warm or hot.

Note: This recipe can
be made up to 3 weeks
in advance and stored
in the freezer.

*Clockwise from top: Cowboy Dogs, Ham and
Pineapple Pinwheels, Chicken Pocket Cones.*

Sesame Cheese Twists and Knots

Preparation time:
  10 minutes
Cooking time:
  10 minutes
Makes about 24

1 *sheet ready-rolled puff pastry*
1 *egg, beaten*
20 g *grated Cheddar cheese*
1 *tablespoon sesame seeds*

1 Preheat oven to moderately hot 210°C. Brush a 32 x 28 cm oven tray with melted butter or oil.
2 Cut the pastry sheet in half, then across width into 2 cm strips.
3 Twist half of the pastry strips 3 times each, and place onto prepared tray. Tie each of the remaining strips into simple knots. Place onto prepared tray.
4 Brush pastry lightly with beaten egg and sprinkle with cheese and sesame seeds. Bake for 10 minutes, or until puffed and golden. Cool on a wire rack.

Note: Sesame Cheese Twists and Knots can be prepared up to 3 days in advance. Store in an airtight container in a cool, dry place.

HINT
For a tasty variation on this recipe, sprinkle pastry shapes with poppy seeds and sea salt. Make a sweet version by cutting pastry into longer strips and forming bows. Sprinkle with sugar and cinnamon and bake as above.

Sesame Cheese Twists and Knots.

1. *For Sesame Cheese Twists and Knots: Cut the pastry into 2 cm strips.*

2. *Twist half the strips and tie remaining strips into simple knots.*

3. Place the shapes onto baking tray and brush with beaten egg.

4. Carefully lift cooked pastries onto a wire rack to cool.

17

Mini Spring Rolls

Preparation Time:
 40 minutes
Cooking Time:
 15 minutes
Makes 16

8 large spring roll
 wrappers
2 spring onions, finely
 chopped
1/3 cup finely chopped
 green capsicum
50 g bean sprouts
6 medium green king
 prawns, peeled,
 deveined and finely
 chopped
1 teaspoon grated ginger
1 teaspoon sherry
2 teaspoons soy sauce
oil for deep frying
sweet dipping sauce,
 to serve

1 Cut each wrapper in
half diagonally. Cover
with a damp cloth.
2 Combine the onion,
capsicum, sprouts,
prawns, ginger, sherry
and soy in a medium
mixing bowl. Stir until
well combined.
3 Place 2 teaspoons of
the mixture onto each
wrapper at the base of
triangle. Fold in edges;
roll up towards point.
Brush end with water;
roll and press to seal.
4 Heat the oil in a deep
heavy-based pan.
Working in batches,
gently lower rolls into
moderately hot oil.
Cook over medium-
high heat until golden
and crisp. Drain on
absorbent paper; keep
warm. Repeat with
remaining spring rolls.
Serve hot with a sweet
sauce for dipping.

Meatballs

Preparation time:
 15 minutes
Cooking time:
 10 minutes
Makes about 25

375 g beef mince
1 small onion, finely
 chopped
1/2 cup fresh breadcrumbs
1 tablespoon tomato
 paste
1 teaspoon
 Worcestershire sauce
1 egg, lightly beaten
2 tablespoons oil

1 Place all ingredients
except the oil in a large
mixing bowl. Using
hands, mix until well
combined. Shape level
tablespoons into balls.
2 Heat oil in a large,
shallow pan. Add
meatballs and cook
over medium heat,
shaking pan often, for
10 minutes or until
mince is cooked and
meatballs are evenly
browned. Drain on
absorbent paper. Serve
hot or cold.

Note: Meatballs can be
cooked up to 3 days in
advance. Store, covered,
in the refrigerator.
Reheat in a moderate
180°C oven.

Fishermen's Burgers

Preparation time:
 15 minutes
Cooking time:
 15 minutes
Makes 6

6 fish fingers
3 rashers bacon, cut
 in half
6 dinner rolls, halved
6 small lettuce leaves
3 cheese slices, halved
6 teaspoons mayonnaise
potato chips, to serve

1 Preheat oven to
moderate 180°C. Wrap
each fish finger in a
piece of bacon, tucking
ends underneath. Place
on an oven tray and
bake for 15 minutes.
2 To assemble burgers,
place a lettuce leaf on
one half of each roll.
Top with cheese, a fish
finger, mayonnaise and
remaining rolls. Serve
hot, with potato chips.

*Clockwise from top: Fishermen's Burgers,
Meatballs and Mini Spring Rolls.*

Mini Pizzas

Preparation Time:
  40 minutes
Cooking Time:
  10 minutes
Makes 40

2 *cups self-raising flour*
100 *g butter, chopped*
1/2 *cup buttermilk*

Topping
2 *tablespoons tomato*
  paste
1 *stick cabanossi, thinly*
  sliced
1 *small onion, sliced*
10 *cherry tomatoes,*
  thinly sliced
6 *cheese slices, cut into*
  3 cm rounds

1 Preheat oven to
moderate 180°C. Line
two 32 x 28 cm oven
trays with foil. Brush
with melted butter or oil.
2 Place flour and
butter in food processor
bowl. Using the pulse
action, press button for
30 seconds or until
mixture is a fine crumbly
texture. Add buttermilk,
process for 30 seconds
or until the mixture
comes together. Knead
dough gently on a
lightly-floured surface
until smooth.
3 Roll the dough out to
3 mm thick. Cut into
rounds using a 5 cm
cutter. Place the rounds
onto prepared tray.

4 Spread tomato paste
evenly over pizza bases.
Arrange the cabanossi,
onion and tomato slices
evenly over bases; top
with cheese. Bake for
10 minutes or until crisp.
Serve hot or warm.

Note: Mini Pizzas can
be made up to 3 weeks
ahead. Freeze uncooked;
bake without thawing.

Ham and Cheese Balls

Preparation Time:
  10 minutes
Cooking Time:
  1 minute
Makes about 24

1/2 *cup sesame seeds*
100 *g soft cream cheese*
100 *g ham, finely*
  chopped
50 *g tasty cheese, grated*

1 Spread sesame seeds
on an oven tray. Toast
under a hot grill for a
few seconds or until
golden. Pour onto a
plate to cool. Set aside.
2 Place cream cheese
into a medium mixing

bowl and mash with a
fork. Add the ham and
grated cheese, mix to
combine. Using hands,
roll heaped teaspoons of
mixture into balls.
3 Roll balls in sesame
seeds. Refrigerate for
1 hour before serving.

Avocado Dip

Preparation time:
  10 minutes
Cooking time:
  Nil
Makes about 1 cup

250 *g soft cream cheese*
2 *small ripe avocados*
3 *teaspoons lemon juice*
1/4 *teaspoon onion*
  powder
cayenne pepper
corn chips, to serve
mixed vegetable sticks,
  such as carrot, celery
  and cucumber, to serve

1 Place cream cheese in
a medium mixing bowl.
Peel and remove stone
from avocados. Mash
flesh and add to cheese
with lemon juice, onion
powder and cayenne
pepper to taste. Stir
until well combined.
2 Cover and place in
refrigerator until ready
to serve. Serve chilled,
with corn chips and
mixed vegetable sticks.

Clockwise from top: Mini Pizzas,
Ham and Cheese Balls and Avocado Dip.

Chicken Nuggets

Preparation Time:
  20 minutes
Cooking Time:
  15 minutes
Makes 34

375 g chicken thigh
  fillets, roughly
  chopped
1 egg, lightly beaten
1 tablespoon chopped
  fresh chives
1/4 teaspoon sesame oil
2 teaspoons plum sauce
1 teaspoon soy sauce
1 cup cornflake crumbs
sweet and sour or extra
  plum sauce, for dipping

1 Preheat oven to
moderate 180°C. Line a
32 x 28 cm oven tray
with foil. Brush with
melted butter or oil.
2 Place chicken, beaten
egg, chives, sesame oil
and sauces in a food
processor bowl. Using
the pulse action, press
button 40 seconds or
until mixture is smooth.
3 Using hands, shape
heaped teaspoons of
mixture into balls. Roll
balls in crumbs. Place
nuggets onto prepared
tray. Bake for 15 minutes
or until golden and
crisp. Serve hot with
sweet and sour or extra
plum sauce for dipping.

Note: Chicken nuggets
can be prepared and
cooked up to 3 weeks
in advance. Cool and
freeze in an airtight
container. Reheat just
before serving.

Cheese and Bacon Tarts

Preparation Time:
  30 minutes
Cooking Time:
  15 minutes
Makes 18

2 sheets ready-rolled
  shortcrust pastry
2 rashers bacon, finely
  chopped
1 small onion, finely
  chopped
1/2 cup cream
1 egg
1/2 teaspoon German
  mustard
1/2 cup grated Cheddar
  cheese

1 Preheat oven to
moderate 180°C. Brush
two shallow 12-cup
patty tins with melted
butter or oil.
2 Lay out pastry on a
lightly-floured surface.
Cut out 18 rounds with
a 7 cm fluted cutter. Ease
the pastry rounds into
patty tins. Sprinkle the
chopped bacon and
onion evenly over pastry.

3 Combine cream, egg
and mustard in a small
mixing bowl. Whisk
until smooth. Spoon
1 teaspoon of mixture
into each pastry case.
Sprinkle with grated
cheese. Bake 15 minutes
or until golden and
crisp. Serve warm or hot.

Note: For Cheese and
Salmon Tarts, substitute
1/3 cup drained and
flaked tinned salmon
for the chopped bacon.

Zebra Sandwiches

Preparation time:
  10 minutes
Cooking time:
  Nil
Makes 8 small
  sandwiches

4 slices day-old bread
1 tablespoon butter
1 tablespoon yeast
  extract or hazelnut
  spread

1 Spread 3 slices of
bread with butter and
either yeast extract or
hazelnut spread. Stack
slices, spread side up.
Top with the plain slice.
Press down gently.
2 Using a sharp knife,
cut crusts neatly from
bread. Cut the stack in
half to make rectangles,
then slice each rectangle
crossways into four
Zebra Sandwiches.

Chicken Nuggets (left), Cheese and
Bacon Tarts (right).

23

Tiny Tuna Baskets

Preparation time:
 15 minutes
Cooking time:
 15 minutes
Makes 24

6 slices stale white bread
20 g butter, melted
180 g can tuna in brine
3 tablespoons cheese
 spread
1 tablespoon chopped
 fresh parsley
6 cherry tomatoes,
 quartered

1 Preheat oven to
moderate 180°C.
2 Remove crusts from
bread. Flatten slices with
a rolling pin; brush each
side lightly with melted
butter. Cut each slice into
quarters. Press into two
12-cup mini muffin tins
or patty tins. Bake for
15 minutes or until crisp
and golden. Let cool.
3 Place tuna in a bowl.
Break up gently with a
fork. Add cheese spread
and parsley and stir until
well combined. Close to
serving, place a teaspoon
of mixture in each case.
Garnish with tomato.

Note: The bread cases
can be made up to one
week ahead. Store in an
airtight container.

Chicken Satay with Peanut Sauce

Preparation time:
 15 minutes
Cooking time:
 15 minutes
Makes 12

500 g chicken fillets,
 cut in thin strips
1 tablespoon oil
1 tablespoon honey
1 tablespoon soy sauce

Peanut Sauce
1/2 cup smooth peanut
 butter
1 tablespoon soy sauce
1/4 teaspoon onion flakes
1/2 cup water
1/2 teaspoon sugar
1 teaspoon sweet chilli
 sauce (optional)

1 Thread chicken onto
skewers. Combine oil,
honey and soy sauce and
brush over chicken. Place
chicken on lightly oiled
grill tray. Cook under
medium heat 10 minutes
or until tender and well-
browned, brushing with
oil mixture several times.
2 Serve Chicken Satay
Sticks warm with Peanut
Sauce for dipping.
3 To make Peanut
Sauce, place all sauce
ingredients in a small
pan. Stir over medium
heat until smooth.

Clockwise from top: Chicken Satay with Peanut Sauce,
 Tiny Tuna Baskets and Zebra Sandwiches (p. 23).

Savoury Filo Rolls

Preparation time:
  20 minutes
Cooking time:
  15 minutes
Makes 16

1 tablespoon oil
1 small onion, finely
  chopped
450 g beef mince
2 tablespoons tomato
  paste
16 sheets filo pastry
40 g butter, melted

1 Preheat oven to moderate 180°C. Brush a 32 x 28 cm oven tray with melted butter or oil.
2 Heat oil in a heavy-based pan; add onion and mince. Cook over medium heat 10 minutes or until well browned and all the liquid has evaporated. Use a fork to break up any lumps. Stir in tomato paste.
3 Place 1 sheet of filo pastry onto the work surface. Brush half the sheet with melted butter and fold over to form a rough square. Place a level teaspoon of meat mixture in the centre of square, 2 cm from front edge. Roll over once, fold sides in and roll to end. Brush the top and sides with melted butter.

Repeat with remaining meat and pastry.
4 Place onto prepared tray. Bake 15-20 minutes or until crisp and golden. Serve warm.

Mini Chicken Pasties

Preparation time:
  15 minutes
Cooking time:
  10 minutes
Makes 24

1 tablespoon oil
350 g chicken mince
1/2 cup frozen diced
  vegetables
lemon pepper
4 sheets ready-rolled
  puff pastry
1 egg, beaten

1 Preheat oven to moderate 180°C. Brush a 32 x 28 cm oven tray with melted butter or oil.
2 Heat oil in a medium heavy-based pan; add chicken mince. Stir over medium heat 5 minutes or until cooked. Use a fork to break up any lumps. Remove from heat; stir in vegetables and pepper to taste.
3 Lay out pastry on a lightly-floured surface. Cut into rounds with an 8 cm cutter. Place a level teaspoon of mixture

onto each pastry round. Fold rounds in half, press edges together. Place pasties onto the prepared tray and brush lightly with beaten egg. Bake for 10 minutes or until lightly golden.

Note: Mini Chicken Pasties can be cooked and frozen for up to 2 months in an airtight container. Thaw in the refrigerator; reheat in a warm oven 10 minutes.

Devon Swags

Preparation time:
  15 minutes
Cooking time:
  Nil
Makes 12

6 slices wholemeal bread
6 cheese sticks
6 slices devon
12 chives
tomato sauce, to serve

1 Remove crusts from bread and flatten with a rolling pin. Place a slice of devon on each piece of bread, then a cheese stick close to one edge. Roll up tightly.
2 Tie 2 chives around each roll, a quarter of the way in from each of the ends.
3 Cut rolls in half so that the chive tie is in the centre of each Swag. Serve with tomato sauce.

Clockwise from top left: Mini Chicken Pasties, Savoury Filo Rolls and Devon Swags.

Sweet Things

Among this selection of delightful birthday treats, sweets, small cakes, slices and biscuits you'll be sure to find just the right dishes to complement your other party fare. Many children think chocolates and cakes are the yummiest things about birthday parties and will eat them exclusively. To get around this, serve the savoury food first, then bring out the sweets. Remember to top up the drinks, too.

Martians

Preparation Time:
  15 minutes + 30
  minutes refrigeration
Cooking Time:
  15 minutes
Makes 24

125 g butter
½ cup caster sugar
1 egg
1¾ cups plain flour

Icing
1 cup icing sugar
3 teaspoons hot water
*4 drops green food
  colouring*
*1 packet liquorice
  allsorts, thinly sliced,
  to decorate*

1 Using electric beaters, beat butter, sugar and egg in a medium bowl until light and creamy.
2 Add flour to bowl. Using hands, press the mixture together to form a soft dough. Turn onto a lightly-floured surface, knead 2 minutes or until smooth. Leave, covered with plastic wrap, in the refrigerator 30 minutes.
3 Preheat oven to moderate 180°C. Brush a 32 x 28 cm biscuit tray with melted butter or oil. Roll dough to 5 mm thickness. Cut into shapes using an 8 cm gingerbread cutter. Place onto prepared tray and bake for 15 minutes or until lightly golden. Lift off and cool on wire rack.
4 Dip the front of each biscuit into Icing to coat. Hold over bowl to allow excess to drain

Chocolate Haystacks (p. 30) (top), Martians (bottom).

away. While icing is still soft, decorate with the allsorts. Repeat with the remaining biscuits. Biscuits can be made up to 7 days ahead. Store iced biscuits up to 2 days in an airtight container.

5 To make Icing: Place icing sugar in medium bowl. Add water and the green colouring; stir until well combined.

Chocolate Haystacks

Preparation Time:
  30 minutes
Cooking Time:
  10 minutes
Makes 40

2 cups sugar
1/3 cup cocoa
1/2 cup milk
125 g butter, chopped
3 cups rolled oats
1 1/2 cups shredded
  coconut

1 Combine sugar and cocoa in a large heavy-based pan. Add the milk and butter. Stir over low heat without boiling until butter has melted and sugar has completely dissolved. Bring the mixture to a full rolling boil, stirring constantly; remove from heat immediately. Add the rolled oats and shredded coconut, stir until well combined.

2 Working quickly, drop heaped teaspoons of chocolate mixture onto greaseproof paper. Allow to set. Store in an airtight container in a cool, dry place.

Note: For easier handling, spoon the hot chocolate mixture into paper patty cases.

Orange Fairy Cakes

Preparation Time:
  25 minutes
Cooking Time:
  10 minutes
Makes 36

125 g butter
3/4 cup caster sugar
2 eggs, lightly beaten
orange colour and
  essence
1 1/2 cups self-raising flour
1/2 teaspoon ground
  nutmeg
1/2 cup milk

Icing
125 g cream cheese
1/4 cup icing sugar, sifted
2 teaspoons grated
  orange rind
1 teaspoon honey
1 teaspoon orange juice

1 Preheat oven to moderate 180°C. Line three deep 12-cup patty tins with paper cases.

2 Using electric beaters, beat butter and sugar in small mixing bowl until light and creamy. Add eggs gradually, beating thoroughly after each addition. Add a few drops of orange colour and essence; beat until just combined.

3 Transfer the mixture to a large mixing bowl. Using a metal spoon, fold in the sifted flour and ground nutmeg alternately with milk. Stir until just combined and mixture is smooth.

4 Spoon tablespoons of mixture into prepared tins. Bake for 10 minutes or until a skewer comes out clean when inserted in centre of cakes.

5 Leave patty cakes for 5 minutes before turning onto a wire rack to cool. When cool, spread Icing on cakes using a flat-bladed knife. Store patty cakes in the freezer for up to 4 weeks. Iced cakes will keep up to 2 days in an airtight container.

6 To make Icing: Beat cream cheese in a small mixing bowl until soft and creamy. Add the remaining ingredients, beating for 3 minutes or until the mixture is smooth and fluffy.

Orange Fairy Cakes.

Peanut Butter Fudge

Preparation Time:
  15 minutes
Cooking Time:
  25 minutes
Makes about 25 pieces

2 cups sugar
3/4 cup milk
2 tablespoons liquid
  glucose
3 tablespoons peanut
  butter
1 teaspoon imitation
  vanilla essence

1 Line a 20 cm square cake tin with aluminium foil, brush foil with melted butter or oil.
2 Combine sugar, milk and glucose in a medium heavy-based pan. Stir over medium heat until sugar has completely dissolved. Brush sugar crystals from sides of pan with a wet pastry brush. Bring to the boil and reduce heat slightly. Boil without stirring for about 20 minutes. Remove from heat immediately.
3 Let mixture cool in pan to lukewarm; add the peanut butter and vanilla essence. Using a wooden spoon, beat until creamy. Pour into prepared tin and cut into squares when set.

Fruit Jelly Shapes

Preparation Time:
  15 minutes +
  overnight refrigeration
Cooking Time:
  5 minutes
Serves 6-8

2 cups orange juice
2 tablespoons sugar
1/4 cup gelatine

1 Line base and sides of an 18 x 27cm oblong cake tin with aluminium foil. Brush with oil.
2 Combine juice and sugar in medium heavy-based pan. Sprinkle the gelatine over. Stir over low heat without boiling until sugar and gelatine have completely dissolved. Bring to boil, boil 1 minute. Remove from heat immediately. Pour mixture into the prepared tin. (Strain if the mixture is lumpy.) Refrigerate overnight.
3 Turn jelly out of tin. Cut a variety of shapes using biscuit cutters. Refrigerate shapes until ready to serve.

Note: For a bright and colourful display, make two or three Fruit Jelly Shapes – try using lime, orange and blackcurrant juices.

Mini Berry Muffins

Preparation Time:
  30 minutes
Cooking Time:
  10 minutes
Makes 40 muffins

2 cups self-raising flour
1/2 teaspoon grated
  orange rind
1/2 cup brown sugar
1 cup milk
1 egg, lightly beaten
125 g butter, melted
300 g packet frozen
  blueberries or
  1 punnet fresh
  blueberries

1 Preheat oven to moderate 180°C. Line two deep 12-cup patty tins with paper cases.
2 Sift flour into a large mixing bowl; add the rind and sugar. Stir to combine. Make a well in the centre. Add the combined milk, egg and butter. Using a wooden spoon, stir until well combined; do not overbeat.
3 Add berries. Lightly fold into the mixture. Spoon tablespoons of mixture into prepared tins. Bake 10 minutes or until golden.
4 Leave muffins in tins 5 minutes before placing on wire rack to cool. Store in an airtight container in a cool, dry place for up to 2 days.

Clockwise from left: Peanut Butter Fudge, Mini Berry Muffins and Fruit Jelly Shapes.

Pretty Party Stars

Preparation Time:
30 minutes + 15
minutes refrigeration
Cooking Time:
10 minutes
Makes 60

125 g butter, softened
1/4 cup caster sugar
1 egg, lightly beaten
2 tablespoons honey
2 teaspoons grated
   lemon rind
2 1/2 cups plain flour
1/2 teaspoon ground
   ginger

Icing

1 3/4 cups icing sugar,
   sifted
2-3 tablespoons lemon
   juice
silver balls, to decorate

1 Preheat oven to
moderate 180°C. Brush
two 32 x 28 cm biscuit
trays with melted butter
or oil, line the base with
paper; grease paper.
2 Using electric beaters,
beat butter and sugar in
small mixing bowl until
light and creamy. Add
the beaten egg; beat well.
Add honey and lemon
rind; beat until combined.
3 Transfer mixture to a
large mixing bowl.
Using a metal spoon,
fold in the combined
sifted flour and ginger.
Stir to form a stiff
dough. Shape the dough
into a ball. Leave dough,
covered with plastic
wrap, in refrigerator for
15 minutes.
4 Roll pastry between
2 sheets of plastic wrap
to 5 mm thickness. Cut
into stars with a 5 cm
cutter. Place pastry
shapes onto prepared
trays. Bake 10 minutes
or until firm and pale
golden. Leave biscuits
on trays for 5 minutes
before turning onto a
wire rack to cool. When
cool, spread with Icing
using a flat-bladed
knife. Decorate with the
silver balls. Store Pretty
Party Stars in an airtight
container between sheets
of greaseproof paper in a
cool, dry place for up to
7 days.
5 To make Icing:
Combine the sifted icing
sugar and just enough of
the lemon juice to form a
spreadable glaze.

HINT
Most children love
to eat sweets, but if
there is a health
reason for sugar not
being allowed try
these alternatives:
small boxes of
sultanas or raisins;
dried apples, apricots,
paw paw or mango;
dried banana chips.
Older children enjoy
shelling peanuts,
walnuts and almonds.

Pretty Party Stars.

*1. For Pretty Party Stars: Add honey and
lemon rind to batter, beat until combined.*

*2. Using a metal spoon, fold in combined
flour and ground ginger.*

3. Roll out pastry and cut into stars with a 5cm cutter.

4. Using a flat-bladed knife, spread biscuits with icing.

Cornflake Crunchies

Preparation Time:
  20 minutes
Cooking Time:
  10 minutes
Makes 24

100 g butter
¼ cup honey
2 tablespoons brown
  sugar
2 cups cornflakes
2 tablespoons chopped
  glacé cherries
2 tablespoons chopped
  mixed nuts (optional)

1 Line two 12-cup patty tins with paper patty cases.
2 Combine the butter, honey and sugar in a small heavy-based pan. Stir over low heat without boiling until the butter has melted and sugar is completely dissolved. Bring to boil; reduce heat. Simmer for 5 minutes. Remove from heat immediately.
3 Combine cornflakes, cherries, nuts (if using) and butter mixture in a medium mixing bowl. Spoon the mixture into patty cases. Refrigerate until set, about 1 hour. Store in an airtight container in refrigerator for up to 2 days.

Beach Baby Jellies

Preparation Time:
  20 minutes +
  overnight refrigeration
Cooking Time:
  Nil
Makes 12

1 x 85 g packet blue
  jelly crystals
1 cup boiling water
12 jelly babies
2 tablespoons fine
  biscuit crumbs
12 lifesaver lollies
12 coloured paper
  parasols

1 Line a 12-cup patty tin with two layers of paper patty cases.
2 Combine blue jelly crystals and water in a jug. Stir until all the crystals have dissolved. Leave until cool.
3 Pour jelly into patty cases to three-quarters full. Refrigerate overnight.
4 Sprinkle the crushed biscuit crumbs over half of each jelly. Lay a jelly baby on the crumbs. Lean a lifesaver lolly against the edge of case and place a parasol in the centre of each jelly. Serve immediately.

Note: Use green jelly crystals if blue crystals are not available.

Cornflake Crunchies (left), Beach Baby Jellies (right).

Cheeky Pikelet Faces

Preparation Time:
  20 minutes
Cooking Time:
  30 minutes
Makes 24

*220 g packet pikelet mix
60 g dark chocolate,
  chopped
butter for greasing*

1 Make up the pikelet mix according to the instructions on packet. Leave the mixture to stand for 10 minutes.
2 Place chocolate in a small heatproof bowl. Stand over a pan of simmering water. Stir until chocolate has melted and is smooth. Spoon chocolate into a small paper icing bag, (see Hint), seal open end. Snip tip off bag.

3 Heat a small amount of butter in a large heavy-based frypan over medium heat. Pipe a small face with the chocolate on the base of the pan. Spoon a tablespoon of pikelet mixture over the face. Cook until bubbles appear on the surface; about 30 seconds. Turn and cook other side.
4 Remove from pan; repeat with remaining chocolate and mixture. Serve warm or cold.

HINT

To make a paper icing bag, cut a 25 cm square of greaseproof paper. Fold in half to make a triangle. With the long side at the bottom roll a corner to the centre and tape in place. Wrap the other side around the back and tape in place.

Cheeky Pikelet Faces.

1. For Cheeky Pikelet Faces: Make pikelet mix according to packet instructions.

2. Make a small paper icing bag, spoon chocolate in and seal.

3. *Pipe a small face with the chocolate onto the base of the pan.*

4. *Working quickly, spoon 1 tablespoon of mixture over the face.*

Chocolate-Chip Shortbread

Preparation Time:
  40 minutes
Cooking Time:
  40 minutes
Makes 30

250 g butter, softened
1/2 cup icing sugar
1 tablespoon drinking
  chocolate
2 cups plain flour
1/2 cup milk
1/2 cup milk choc-bits
30 milk choc-bits, extra

1 Preheat oven to slow 150°C. Brush two 32 x 28 cm oven trays with melted butter or oil, line base with paper; grease paper.
2 Using electric beaters, beat butter and sugar in small mixing bowl until light and creamy. Add drinking chocolate; beat until combined.
3 Transfer mixture to a large mixing bowl. Using a metal spoon, fold in the sifted flour alternately with the milk. Stir until just combined and mixture is almost smooth. Add choc-bits. Using floured hands, roll tablespoons of the mixture into balls. Place an extra choc-bit on each. Bake 40 minutes or until firm. Leave to cool on trays. Store in an airtight container for up to 3 weeks.

Jelly Slice

Preparation Time:
  15 minutes +
  overnight setting
Cooking Time:
  Nil
Makes 30

2 x 85 g packets
  strawberry jelly crystals
500 ml boiling water
15 coloured 9 x 5 cm
  wafers

1 Line a shallow 27 x 18 cm oblong cake tin with aluminium foil.
2 Combine the jelly crystals and water in a jug. Stir until the crystals have dissolved. Pour into the prepared tin. Refrigerate overnight.
3 Using foil, lift jelly from tin. Peel foil back from sides of jelly. Cut wafers in half crossways. Place half the wafers on the jelly. Using them as a guide, cut jelly to fit. Sandwich jelly squares between 2 wafers, and cut in half crossways.

Note: Do not refrigerate assembled Jelly Slices as the wafers will soften.

Jelly Slice (top), Chocolate-Chip Shortbread (bottom).

Chocolate-Chip Crackles

Preparation Time:
  20 minutes
Cooking Time:
  5 minutes
Makes 24

3 cups Rice Bubbles
1/4 cup cocoa
1 1/4 cups icing sugar
1/2 cup sultanas
3/4 cup desiccated
  coconut
200 g white vegetable
  shortening
1/3 cup choc bits

1 Line two deep
12-cup patty tins with
paper cases. Place Rice
Bubbles in large mixing
bowl. Add combined
sifted cocoa and icing
sugar; mix well. Stir in
sultanas and coconut.
2 Place shortening in
small heavy-based pan.
Heat gently until melted;
stir into crackle mixture.
3 Spoon into prepared
cases. Sprinkle with
choc bits. Refrigerate
until set. Store in airtight
container in refrigerator
for up to 5 days.

Tiny Strawberry Tarts

Preparation Time:
  20 minutes + 30
  minutes refrigeration
Cooking Time:
  20 minutes
Makes 24

1/2 cup plain flour
40 g butter
1 tablespoon sugar
1 tablespoon water
2 tablespoons custard
  powder
1 tablespoon sugar, extra
3/4 cup milk
12 small strawberries,
  halved
2 tablespoons baby
  apple gel

1 Sift the flour into a
medium mixing bowl;
add the chopped butter.
Using fingertips, rub
butter into the flour for
3 minutes or until
mixture is a fine,
crumbly texture. Stir in
the sugar. Add almost
all the water, mix to a
firm dough, adding
more water if necessary.
Turn onto a lightly-
floured surface, knead
2 minutes until smooth.
Leave, covered with
plastic wrap, in the
refrigerator 30 minutes.
2 Preheat oven to
moderate 180°C.

Roll the pastry out to
2 mm thickness, and
cut into rounds using a
5 cm cutter. Press the
rounds into mini muffin
tins or small patty tins.
Bake for 15 minutes or
until lightly golden. Set
aside to cool.

*Tiny Strawberry Tarts and
Chocolate-Chip Crackles.*

3 In a small heavy-based pan, combine custard powder and sugar. Add enough of the milk to make a smooth paste. Add remaining milk and stir over low heat until mixture boils and thickens. Set aside.

4 To assemble tarts, place a teaspoon of cooled custard into each case. Top with half a strawberry, and brush with warmed apple gel.

Note: Tart cases can be made up to 7 days ahead and stored in an airtight container. Custard can be made up to 12 hours ahead, and stored, covered with plastic wrap, in the refrigerator. Assemble the tarts up to 4 hours before serving. Store in refrigerator.

Jelly-Dipped Cupcakes

Preparation Time:
  20 minutes
Cooking Time:
  15 minutes
Makes 30

340 g packet buttercake
  mix
85 g packet red jelly
  crystals
85 g packet green jelly
  crystals
400 ml boiling water
2 cups desiccated
  coconut

1 Preheat oven to moderate 180°C. Line two 15-cup patty tins with paper patty cases.
2 Make up buttercake according to the instructions on packet. Place level tablespoons of mixture into each case. Bake 15 minutes or until lightly golden and springy to the touch. Remove paper cases and place onto a wire rack to cool.
2 Place jelly crystals into separate small mixing bowls. Pour half the boiling water into each bowl and stir to dissolve crystals. Allow to cool, but not set.
3 Working one at a time, dip each cake into either green or red jelly, then roll in the coconut. Turn cakes upside down and leave to set. Repeat with remaining cakes. Refrigerate overnight to set. Serve chilled.

Psychedelic Fairy Bread

Preparation Time:
  10 minutes
Cooking Time:
  Nil
Serves 8

8 slices white bread
2 tablespoons butter
sprinkles of different
  colours

1 Spread bread with butter and remove crusts. Place a biscuit cutter or egg ring on the centre of the slice as a guide. Sprinkle a light, even coating of one colour of sprinkles inside the guide, and a contrasting colour on the outside.
2 Remove cutter; press sprinkles gently with fingers to secure. Fairy bread can be made up to 2 hours ahead. Store in refrigerator.

Note: Spirals or stripes of coloured sprinkles are also very effective.

Psychedelic Fairy Bread (left), Jelly-Dipped Cupcakes (right).

Meringue Snails and Worms

Preparation Time:
  30 minutes
Cooking Time:
  35 minutes
Makes about 30

2 egg whites
1/2 cup caster sugar
2 tablespoons icing
  sugar
2 teaspoons lemon juice
food colouring, optional
coloured sprinkles,
  optional
sweets, optional, for
  decorating

1 Preheat oven to slow
150°C. Brush two
32 x 28 cm oven trays
with melted butter or
oil. Line base with paper;
grease paper. Dust lightly
with sifted cornflour;
shake off excess.
2 Place egg whites in a
small, dry mixing bowl.
Using electric beaters,
beat the whites until
soft peaks form.
3 Add sugar gradually,
beating constantly until
mixture is thick and
glossy. Add icing sugar,
lemon juice and a few
drops of colouring, if
using. Beat a further
3 minutes or until all
the sugar is dissolved.
4 Spoon mixture into a
large piping bag, fitted
with a plain round
nozzle; pipe worm and

snail shapes onto the
prepared trays.
Decorate shapes with
sprinkles or use sweets
for eyes and teeth. Bake
35 minutes or until pale
and crisp. Remove from
the oven, cool on trays.
Store meringues, lightly
packed or in a single
layer, in an airtight
container in a cool, dry
place for up to 3 weeks.

Cherry and Coconut Squares

Preparation Time:
  30 minutes
Cooking Time:
  25÷30 minutes
Makes 20 squares

2 eggs, separated
2/3 cup icing sugar
1/3 cup desiccated
  coconut
1/2 cup shredded coconut
1/4 cup chopped glacé
  cherries
1/2 cup ground almonds
1/4 cup rice flour
2 teaspoons grated
  lemon rind
2 tablespoons shredded
  coconut, extra

1 Preheat oven to
moderate 180°C. Brush
a deep 20 cm square
cake tin with melted
butter or oil. Line base
and sides with paper;
grease paper.
2 Place egg whites in
small, dry mixing bowl.
Using electric beaters,
beat egg whites until
soft peaks form.
3 Add sugar gradually,
beating 5 minutes or
until mixture is thick.
Add yolks; beat a
further 3 minutes.
4 Transfer mixture to
a large mixing bowl.
Using a metal spoon,
fold in the coconut,
cherries, almonds, rice
flour and rind. Stir until
just combined and the
mixture almost smooth.
5 Spoon mixture into
prepared tin; smooth
surface. Sprinkle with
extra coconut. Bake
25-30 minutes or until
golden and a skewer
comes out clean when
inserted into the centre.
Leave in tin 5 minutes
before turning onto a
wire rack to cool. When
cool, cut into squares
with a sharp knife. Store
in an airtight container
in a cool, dry place for
up to 2 weeks.

Note: Replace cherries
with other glacé fruit,
if desired.

Meringue Snails and Worms (top), Cherry
and Coconut Squares (bottom).

Popcorn Pops

Preparation Time:
  15 minutes
Cooking Time:
  15 minutes
Makes 6

1 tablespoon oil
¼ cup popping corn
¾ cup sugar
25 g butter
¼ cup water
4 drops red or green
  food colouring
6 wooden icy-pole sticks

1 Heat oil in a large pan. Add corn, cover and cook over medium heat. Hold the lid tightly, shaking pan occasionally. Cook until the popping stops. Put popcorn in a large bowl; set aside.
2 Combine the sugar, butter and water in a small heavy-based pan. Stir over medium heat without boiling until sugar has completely dissolved. Brush sugar crystals from the sides of the pan with a wet pastry brush. Bring to boil; boil without stirring for 5 minutes. Remove from heat, stir in food colouring.
3 Pour the syrup over the popcorn. Using two metal spoons, combine thoroughly. Allow the mixture to cool until just possible to handle. With oiled hands and working quickly, press the popcorn firmly into roughly ball shapes around the top of each icy-pole stick. Serve on the day of making.

Marshmallow Slice

Preparation Time:
  10 minutes
Cooking Time:
  5 minutes
Makes 54 small squares

2½ cups Rice Bubbles
100 g pink
  marshmallows, chopped
100 g white
  marshmallows, chopped
1 cup desiccated
  coconut
125 g white vegetable
  shortening
125 g dark cooking
  chocolate, chopped

1 Line a shallow 27 x 18 cm oblong tin with aluminium foil. Combine the Rice Bubbles, pink and white marshmallows and coconut in a large mixing bowl, make a well in the centre.
2 Place shortening in a small pan and stir over a low heat until melted. Add to bowl. Using a wooden spoon, stir until well combined; do not overbeat. Pour into the prepared tin; leave to set.
3 Place chocolate in a small heatproof bowl. Stand over a pan of simmering water, stir until chocolate has melted and is smooth. Let cool slightly, pour over marshmallow and spread evenly with a flat-bladed knife. Leave to set. Cut into small squares to serve.

Chocolate Dip

Preparation Time:
  5 minutes
Cooking Time:
  Nil
Makes about 2 cups

250 g natural yoghurt
250 g soft cream cheese
⅓ cup chocolate syrup
chopped fruit, to serve,
  marshmallows, to serve

1 Combine yoghurt and cream cheese in a medium bowl. Using a wooden spoon, beat until mixture is smooth and free from lumps.
2 Add chocolate syrup; stir until well combined. Transfer to a serving bowl. Serve with small pieces of seasonal fruit and marshmallows. Chocolate Dip can be made up to 2 hours ahead. Refrigerate until ready to serve.

From top: Marshmallow Slice, Popcorn Pops and Chocolate Dip.

Crunchy-Top Brownies

Preparation Time:
  15 minutes
Cooking Time:
  40 minutes
Makes 25

2/3 cup self-raising flour
1/3 cup plain flour
150 g dark cooking
  chocolate, chopped
2 tablespoons water
100 g butter
1/2 cup caster sugar
2 eggs, lightly beaten
1/3 cup Coco Pops

Icing
1/2 cup icing sugar
60 g butter, softened

1 Preheat oven to
moderate 180°C. Brush
a 20 cm square cake tin
with melted butter or
oil. Cover base with
paper; grease paper.
2 Sift the flours into a
large mixing bowl. Make
a well in the centre.
Combine dark chocolate,
water and butter in a
small pan. Stir over low
heat until chocolate and
butter have melted. Add
sugar and stir until sugar
has dissolved; remove
from heat; leave to cool.
3 Add the chocolate
mixture and the beaten
eggs to dry ingredients.

Using a wooden spoon,
stir until well combined;
do not overbeat.
4 Pour the mixture into
the prepared tin. Bake
for 40 minutes. Leave
to cool in tin.
5 Spread Icing over
brownie base; sprinkle
with Coco Pops and cut
into squares. Store in an
airtight container in the
refrigerator.
6 To make Icing:
Combine the icing sugar
and butter in a small
bowl; beat until smooth.

Pink Marshmallows

Preparation Time:
  25 minutes +
  overnight setting
Cooking Time:
  Nil
Makes 36

1 1/2 cups caster sugar
1/2 cup water
5 teaspoons gelatine
1/2 cup water, extra
1 teaspoon imitation
  vanilla essence
4 drops red food
  colouring
3/4 cup icing sugar

1 Line base and sides
of a shallow 20 x 30 cm
oblong cake tin with
foil; brush the foil with
melted butter or oil.

2 Using electric beaters,
beat sugar and water in
a large mixing bowl for
3 minutes.
3 Combine the gelatine
with water in a small
bowl. Stand bowl in hot
water; stir until gelatine
dissolves. Add to sugar
mixture. Using electric
beaters, beat for 10

Pink Marshmallows (left), Crunchy-
Top Brownies (right).

minutes, until mixture is thick and white. Add vanilla essence and red food colouring and beat until combined.

4 Pour the mixture into prepared tin and spread evenly. Cover loosely with plastic wrap and leave to set overnight at room temperature.

5 Turn marshmallow out of tin, peel off foil and cut into squares. Place icing sugar in a plastic bag; add a few cubes of marshmallow at a time, shake to coat with icing sugar. Store in an airtight container in a cool, dark place for up to 1 week.

HINT

In hot weather, even the most dedicated anti-washers among young guests will appreciate a wet cloth to clean up sticky little hands and faces. Purchased wet paper cloths are convenient.

Icy Treats & Drinks

Being a guest at a children's birthday party can be hot and thirsty work, so refreshing drinks and chilled desserts are always welcome. Offer guests a choice of two drinks, for example our tasty, thirst-quenching Homemade Lemonade and a more substantial creamy one such as Choc-Chip Banana Smoothie. Dress up ice-cream cones, parfaits and sundaes in their party best to please young eyes and palates, too. Serve dishes straight from freezer or refrigerator; keep portions small to suit kid-size appetites.

Caramel Wafer Sundae

Preparation Time:
  20 minutes
Cooking Time:
  5 minutes
Serves 8

16 *scoops vanilla
  ice-cream*
4 *oblong ice-cream
  wafers, cut diagonally*
2 *choc-coated caramel
  fudge bars, chopped*

Caramel Sauce
1/2 *cup (100 g)
  caramel buds*
50 g *butter*
1 *tablespoon brown
  sugar*
1/2 *cup cream*

1 To make Caramel Sauce: Combine the caramel buds, butter, brown sugar and cream in a small heavy-based pan. Stir over medium heat until caramel buds and butter have melted and sugar has completely dissolved. Remove from heat. Cool slightly.
2 Place 2 scoops of ice-cream into each bowl. Pour Caramel Sauce over. Decorate with a wafer triangle and the chopped fudge bars.

Note: Caramel Sauce can be made up to 2 weeks in advance. Store the sauce in an airtight container in the refrigerator. Reheat gently before serving.

*Caramel Wafer Sundae (left), Choc-Chip
Banana Smoothie (p. 54) (right).*

Choc-Chip Banana Smoothie

Preparation Time:
  10 minutes
Cooking Time:
  Nil
Makes 4 cups

1 cup milk
2 large bananas
1/2 cup plain yoghurt
3/4 cup vanilla ice-cream
1 tablespoon chocolate
  topping
2 teaspoons honey
1/2 cup choc-bits
grated chocolate, to
  garnish

1 Place milk, bananas, yoghurt, ice-cream, chocolate topping, honey and choc-bits in food processor bowl. Using the pulse action press button 30 seconds or until the mixture is fairly smooth.
2 Pour the mixture into clear plastic cups. Store, covered, in refrigerator for up to 3 hours. Just before serving, sprinkle with grated chocolate.

Sunburst Parfaits

Preparation Time:
  1/2 hour + 1 hour
  refrigeration
Cooking Time:
  5 minutes
Makes 6

2 tablespoons custard
  powder
1/4 cup caster sugar
1 1/2 cups milk
1/2 cup cream
1 egg yolk
1 teaspoon vanilla
  essence
1 cup (200 g) canned
  apricots, sliced
1 packet orange or
  apricot jelly
1 cup boiling water
whipped cream, to serve
chopped fresh fruit, to
  serve

1 Combine the custard powder and sugar in a medium heavy-based pan. Gradually whisk in the combined milk and cream. Stir over low heat 5 minutes or until mixture boils and thickens. Remove from heat. Whisk in yolk and essence. Pour custard evenly into goblets. Refrigerate until firm.
2 Combine jelly crystals and water in a jug. Stir until all crystals have dissolved. Leave to cool to room temperature.

3 Divide the apricots evenly between goblets; pour jelly evenly over. Refrigerate until set.
4 Just before serving, decorate with whipped cream and fresh fruit.

Note: Serve Sunburst Parfaits in small plastic wine goblets, available from supermarkets.

Apricot Fluff

Preparation Time:
  10 minutes
Cooking Time:
  Nil
Makes 6 cups

1/4 cup ricotta cheese
1/2 cup plain yoghurt
1 tablespoon honey
1 1/2 cups apricot nectar
6 ice cubes
fresh fruit, to garnish
6 paper parasols

1 Place ricotta, yoghurt, honey, nectar and ice cubes in food processor bowl. Using the pulse action, press button for 30 seconds or until mixture is smooth.
2 Pour into 6 clear plastic cups; garnish with fruit and a parasol.

Note: Make Apricot Fluff just before serving as the mixture may separate if left to stand.

Apricot Fluff (left), Sunburst Parfaits (right).

1. For Layered Ice-Cream Cups: Add sugar gradually to beaten eggs.

2. Divide the mixture between 8 large, transparent plastic cups.

3. *Using a metal spoon, fold cream and topping into beaten egg whites.*

4. *Add a few drops of red food colouring to the cream mixture.*

Layered Ice-Cream Cups

Preparation Time:
  1 hour + 5 hours
  freezing + overnight
  freezing
Cooking Time: Nil
Makes 8 large cups

Caramel layer
2 eggs
3/4 cup caster sugar
1 3/4 cups cream
1/4 cup milk
1-2 tablespoons
  caramel flavouring

Chocolate layer
2 egg whites
1/2 cup cream
3 tablespoons chocolate
  topping

Topping
1 1/4 cups cream
2 tablespoons
  blackberry jam
1 tablespoon
  strawberry flavouring
red food colouring

1 To make Caramel layer: Using electric beaters, beat eggs in small mixing bowl for 2 minutes or until thick and pale. Add sugar gradually, beating constantly until dissolved and mixture is pale yellow and glossy. Transfer mixture to a large mixing bowl. Gradually beat in the combined cream and milk. Beat 5 minutes or until mixture begins to thicken. Add caramel flavouring, mix well. Divide mixture evenly between 8 cups. Freeze 5 hours or until firm.
2 To make Chocolate layer: Place egg whites in a small, dry mixing bowl. Using electric beaters, beat until soft peaks form. Using a metal spoon, gradually fold in cream and chocolate topping. Stir until mixture is just combined. Divide the mixture evenly between

the cups. Return to freezer. Freeze overnight.
3 To make Topping: Using electric beaters, beat cream in medium bowl until soft peaks form. Add blackberry jam, flavouring and a few drops of the food colouring. Beat until stiff peaks form. Spoon the mixture into a large piping bag fitted with a star piping nozzle. Pipe swirls onto each ice-cream. Serve immediately.

HINT
Take advantage of seasonal fruits to make a summer party fruit salad. Combine chopped fresh fruit in a large bowl, sprinkle with lemon juice and caster sugar to taste. Cover and refrigerate 2 hours. Serve in a watermelon hollowed out and carved into a boat or basket.

57

Pineapple Cream Crush

Preparation Time:
 5 minutes
Cooking Time:
 Nil
Makes about 1 L

1 x 450 g can crushed
 pineapple
1 cup pineapple juice
200 mL coconut milk
pineapple slices to
 garnish

1 Combine the crushed pineapple and juice in a large jug.
2 Slowly pour in the coconut milk, whisking continually until well blended. To serve, pour into tall glasses over plenty of ice. Garnish with pineapple slices. Serve immediately.

Homemade Lemonade

Preparation Time:
 10 minutes + 2 hours
 standing
Cooking Time:
 5 minutes
Makes 2 L

1 cup sugar
1 cup water
3 tablespoons finely
 grated lemon rind
1 cup lemon juice
1½ L water, extra

1 Combine sugar and water in a small heavy-based pan. Stir over medium heat without boiling until sugar has completely dissolved. Brush sugar crystals from side of pan with a wet pastry brush. Bring to the boil, reduce heat slightly, and boil for 1 minute. Leave to cool.
2 Combine lemon rind, lemon juice and extra water in a large jug and add the cooled syrup. Let stand for 2 hours; strain and refrigerate. Dilute to taste.

Witches' Brew

Preparation Time:
 5 minutes
Cooking Time:
 Nil
Makes 6 cups

600 mL cola drink
6 small scoops vanilla
 ice-cream
3 teaspoons strawberry
 syrup
12 snake lollies, to
 decorate

1 Pour 100 mL of cola into each of six clear plastic cups. Add a scoop of ice-cream to each glass. Stir gently to foam (mixture will 'boil over' if stirred too hard).

2 Drizzle ½ teaspoon of syrup onto each drink. Hang 2 snakes over the side of each cup. Serve immediately.

Sunshine Punch

Preparation Time:
 5 minutes + 1 hour
 refrigeration
Cooking Time:
 Nil
Makes about 2½ L

850 mL can unsweetened
 pineapple juice
3 cups apple juice
450 g can unsweetened
 crushed pineapple
750 mL lemonade or
 dry ginger ale, chilled
mint sprigs and glacé
 cherries, to garnish

1 In a large serving bowl combine the pineapple and apple juices with the crushed pineapple; stir lightly to combine. Cover and refrigerate for 1 hour or until well chilled.
2 Just before serving, add the lemonade or ginger ale to pineapple mixture. Garnish with mint and glacé cherries. Serve immediately.

Note: Substitute orange and mango juice for apple juice, if liked.

Clockwise from top: Homemade Lemonade, Sunshine Punch, Pineapple Cream Crush and Witches' Brew.

Meteor Ice-Cream Cones

Preparation Time:
  20 minutes
Cooking Time:
  5 minutes
Makes 8

150 g dark cooking
  chocolate, chopped
30 g white vegetable
  shortening
8 small round or square
  ice-cream cups
16 scoops ice-cream,
  very cold
200 g packet chocolate
  buttons, to decorate

1 Place chocolate and shortening in a medium heatproof bowl. Stand over pan of simmering water, stir until chocolate and shortening have melted and mixture is smooth. Cool slightly.
2 Place 2 scoops of ice-cream in each ice-cream cup, packing it in firmly. Working one at a time, carefully dip the top of the ice-cream into the warm chocolate mixture. Drain off excess chocolate. While the chocolate is still warm press a few chocolate buttons on to decorate. Repeat with remaining ingredients. Serve immediately.

Tropical Slushy

Preparation Time:
  10 minutes +
  overnight freezing
Cooking Time:
  Nil
Makes 2 litres

450 g can tropical fruit
  salad
450 g can crushed
  pineapple
1 L tropical fruit juice

1 Line a 20 cm square cake tin with foil, extending it over two sides. Pour all ingredients into prepared tin, stir and freeze overnight.
2 Using foil, lift frozen mixture from the tin. Break up ice roughly. Place in food processor or blender (in two batches if necessary) and process until mixture becomes slushy ice.
3 To serve, spoon into tall plastic glasses. Serve Tropical Slushy immediately, with a long spoon in each glass.

Frozen Banana Bites

Preparation Time:
  10 minutes + 2 hours
  freezing
Cooking Time:
  5 minutes
Makes 18

3 large bananas
9 wooden icy-pole sticks
100 g dark cooking
  chocolate, chopped
20 g white vegetable
  shortening

1 Line a 32 x 28 cm oven tray with foil. Cut each banana into 6 pieces. Cut icy-pole sticks in half. Carefully push a half-stick into each piece of banana.
2 Combine chocolate and shortening in a small heatproof bowl. Stand over a pan of simmering water, stir until melted and mixture is smooth.
3 Working one at a time, dip each banana piece into hot chocolate mixture. Drain off any excess chocolate. Place onto prepared tray. Refrigerate until chocolate is set, then store in an airtight container in the freezer at least 2 hours.

Note: Frozen Banana Bites should be eaten on the day they are made.

Clockwise from left: Meteor Ice-Cream Cones, Tropical Slushy and Frozen Banana Bites.

Jaffa Mousse

Preparation Time:
  20 minutes + 1½
  hours refrigeration
Cooking Time:
  Nil
Serves 8

150 g dark cooking
  chocolate, chopped
4 eggs, separated
2 tablespoons caster
  sugar
1 teaspoon grated
  orange rind
⅓ cup cream
1 teaspoon gelatine
1 tablespoon orange
  juice

1 Place chocolate in a small heatproof bowl. Stand over a pan of simmering water, stir until chocolate has melted and mixture is smooth. Cool slightly.
2 Using electric beaters, beat yolks, sugar and rind in a large mixing bowl for 5 minutes until thick and creamy. Beat in the cream and the melted chocolate.
3 Combine the gelatine with juice in a small bowl. Stand bowl in hot water; stir until gelatine dissolves. Add to the chocolate mixture and beat until combined.
4 Place egg whites in a small, dry mixing bowl.

Using electric beaters, beat until firm peaks form. Add to chocolate mixture. Using a metal spoon, fold whites in until well combined. Spoon into small bowls. Refrigerate 1½ hours or until set. Serve cold.

Smart-Alec Split

Preparation Time:
  10 minutes + 30
  minutes refrigeration
  + 1 hour freezing
Cooking Time:
  Nil
Makes 6

500 ml vanilla ice-cream
¼ cup strawberry syrup
3 bananas
6 tablespoons chocolate
  syrup
chocolate buttons, to
  decorate

1 Remove ice-cream from freezer. Leave to soften in refrigerator for 30 minutes. Drizzle the strawberry syrup over ice-cream and swirl through gently with a fork. Return to freezer 1 hour or until frozen.
2 Cut bananas in half lengthways. Place a half in each bowl; top with 2 small scoops ice-cream and chocolate syrup. Top with chocolate buttons. Serve immediately.

Smart-Alec Split (top), Jaffa Mousse (bottom).

Index